JACK VETTRIANO

WOMEN IN LOVE

JACK VETTRIANO

WOMEN IN LOVE

PAVILION

Previous Page: Dance Me To The End of Love

love

- noun

1 an intense feeling of deep affection.
2 a deep romantic or sexual attachment to someone.

I have always sought the company of women over men. This is not purely a sexual endeavour; as companions, they possess a range of qualities that far outweigh those of mere man.

In choosing the paintings for *Women In Love*, I have purposely avoided my femme fatales and their compulsive yet compelling manipulative behaviour. I have chosen those paintings which I think best illustrate my definition of love and contain the aspects of women that draw me in.

'All the rocket ships are climbing through the skies,
the holy books are open wide,
the doctors working day and night,
but they'll never ever find a cure for love.
Ain't no cure for love.'
('Ain't no cure for love' by Leonard Cohen)

The Singing Butler

The Missing Man

Tender Hearts

Elegy for the Dead Admiral

The Shape of
Things to Come

VETTRIANO.

Right Time Right Place

Bad Boy, Good Girl

Dancer in Emerald

The Sun Worshippers

VETTRIANO

Sweet Bird of Youth (Study)

Sweet Bird of Youth

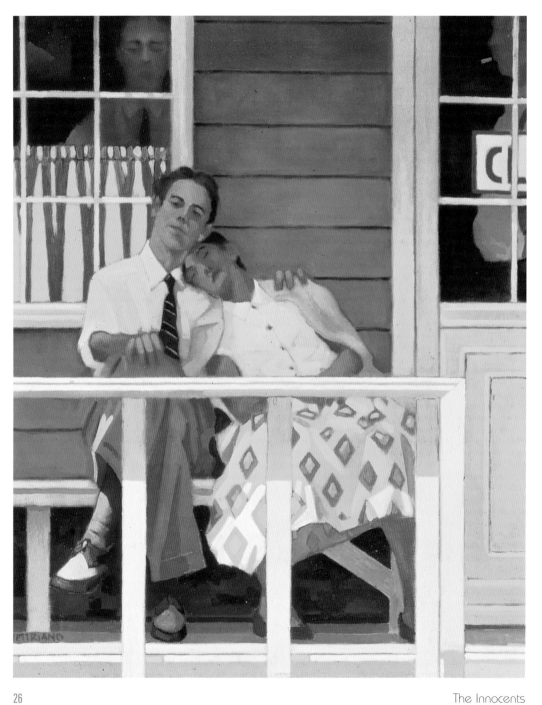

The Innocents

Mr Cool

A Day at the Races

The British Are Coming

Bird On The Wire

The Tourist

Exit Eden

Riviera Retro

Blades

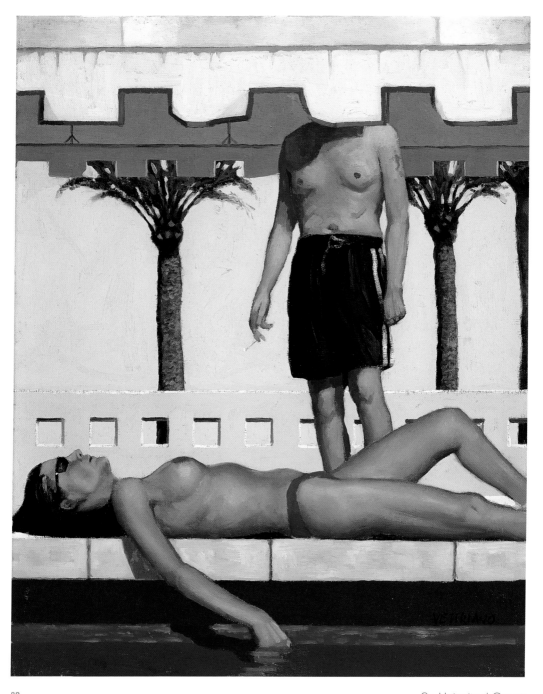

La Fille à la Moto

Her Secret Life

Suddenly One Summer

The Ice Maiden

Café Days

The Man in the Navy Suit

Lunchtime Lovers

Birdy

Queen of the Waltzer

Long Time Gone

The Great Escape

Back Where You Belong

The Railway Station

Angel

The Red Room

The Runaways

56

The Man in the Mirror

Cocktails and Broken Hearts

Betrayal – The First Kiss

Contemplation of Betrayal

The Jazz Singer

The Main Attraction

Shades of Scarlett

Next Up

Dancer Number 7

Betrayal – No Turning Back

Waltzers

Tango Dancers

Dressing to Kill

Just Another Day

Yesterday's Dreams

Portrait in Silver and Maroon

The Model and the Drifter

A Valentine Rose

Models in the Studio II

Tomorrow Never Comes

Winter Light and Lavender

Model in Black

Edinburgh Afternoon

Model in White

One Moment in Time

The Tulip Dress

Table for One

The Letter

Drawing Room, Easterheughs

After the Thrill is Gone

Baby, Bye Bye

Models in the Studio (Study)

Model in Westwood

Only the Deepest Red

Night in The City

After Midnight

Queen of Vanities

Rooms of a Stranger

Welcome to My World

The Arrangement

The Look of Love

The Mark of Cain

Mirror, Mirror

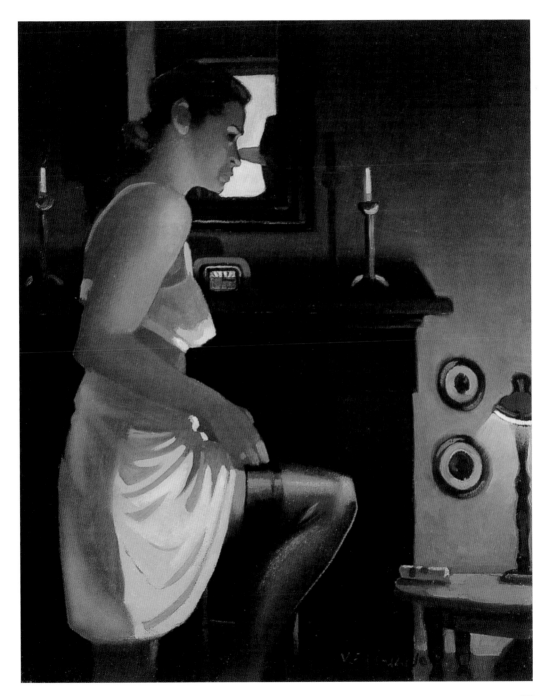

The White Slip

Index of paintings

First published in Great Britain in 2009
by Pavilion

An imprint of the Anova Books Company Ltd
10 Southcombe Street, London W14 0RA

Paintings © Jack Vettriano
Design and layout © Pavilion
Designed by Martin Hendry
Jacket Design by Georgina Hewitt

A CIP catalogue record for this book is available
from the British Library.

ISBN 978 1 86205 855 2

Printed and bound by 1010 Printing International Ltd,
China

10 9 8 7 6 5 4 3 2 1

This book can be ordered direct from the publisher.
Please contact the Marketing Department. But try
your bookshop first.

www.anovabooks.com

For further information on Jack Vettriano please visit
www.jackvettriano.com